BE STILL AND KNOW THAT I AM GOD

"Surviving The Storms of Marriage"

ISBN-13:
978-0692781210 (Personal One Touch Publishing)

ISBN-10:
0692781218

Foreword

In a society that disregards the sacredness of Church also disregards the sacredness of marriage. Marriage is sacred. It is a holy union between a man and a woman. Marriage is a consecrated relationship not only to one another but as unto God. In His design of marriage, He also set it up whereby we would experience some hard times in our adapting to one another and still stay married. The book you are about to read and study together will show you how to stay together even when it's been infidelity in the marriage. It will bear witness that you can always trust God then trust your spouse again. Lady Kathy will share how you can rebuild your trust without checking a cell phone, or searching pockets or reading emails for signs of yet another affair. When you commit your life to Jesus and then your marriage to Him, there's nothing that you and your spouse will face that God will not be right there with you. God is Emmanuel....He is with you......as He was with this couple. Enjoy.

Mrs. Brenda Fruster
WINNERS Worship Center

Acknowledgments

First and foremost, I thank God for giving me the strength, patience, and endurance to survive the storms of marriage. This book would not exist if it had not been for His Grace! I thank my husband Marshall who is the head of my household, my prophet, my priest, and my king. Next to God; there is no one greater than you. I thank my son; Marshall Jr for his very existence and always having a listening ear. I thank my Pastors; Robert & Brenda Fruster for their never-ending support. I thank my mom, my dad and a host of family and friends who are to vast to name. Special thanks to my Editor & Publisher Brenda Dennis; without you; this baby would not have been birth! The encouragement that each of you have imparted is priceless!

Introduction

Marriage is a special bond between two imperfect people coming together to be perfect for each other. Caring for one another and getting to know each other requires a lot of compromise by removing the mask that so many of us wear to cover up who we really are. *"Be Still & Know That I am God-Surviving the Storms of Marriage"* will show you how to get to know the real person, how to let your guard down, and the BIG ONE: Keeping communication open and honest during the ups and the downs.

Father, thank You for guiding me to write a book that is needed by many who make the choice to give up on their marriage. Marriage is a covenant that should be taken seriously by investing in the time to do whatever it takes in a legal and lawful way. Marriage is a lifelong commitment until death separates the covenant agreement. Marriages that are ordained by God should be together for life. Instead, some couples treat marriage like it's just something to do. It is my prayer that this devotional equips every person that reads this book with the tools necessary to love through the good and the bad times. Also, to minister to you as much as it has ministered to me. Holy Spirit, thank you for helping me to be honest and transparent.

I met my husband through a good friend of mine who just so happens to be his sister Daisy. One day while over their house I just so happen to see him. He lived at home because we were teenagers; however, on this day; I saw him and that was history. I knew instantly he was my soulmate. At the age of 13; I was crazy about me some Marshall! Every time I would see him; I would get all giggly. I had the biggest crush on him; even though he never seen me that way or was attracted to me. I remember I would flirt with him when I see him walking to the store. I would ask him to buy me some barbeque chips and cherry vanilla ice-cream. He stayed 7 houses down from me so he had to pass my house to drop off my snacks as he went to his house. We never dated or went out. At the age of 16; he was the first person I kissed. He left to go to trading school in Kentucky and was gone for 2 years. We didn't date or keep up with one another however; my friend was dating his brother. While out shopping during the holidays; I told my friend that I was going to buy Marshall a sweater and give it to him as a Christmas present. On Christmas day, I called and told him I wanted to come over and give him a gift and he said ok. I gave him the sweater, he thanked me for it, and we never spoke or hung out afterwards. The following Christmas will be one I will never forget! My Mom told me that she knew a secret and that I was going to be surprised with a gift from someone I would never expect. I received a call on Christmas from Marshall asking me to meet him at his house. When I arrived; he met me with a gift. Enclosed were 14 karat gold ball earrings. I asked him what made him buy me a gift and he told me that I did something for him that no one has ever done for him before. His family was surprised because they knew the big crush I had on him, yet he never paid no attention to me. On that day, we started dating. I was 23 years old. I often joke with him because I recall that day at the age of 16 when we kissed and he asked me to go in this empty house and get busy. I said no, even though I was crazy about him. I often remind him if I would have 'given up my goodies' he wouldn't have respected me nor would we be together. He was the first person, I kissed and became intimate with. I never knew that it meant something to him until I heard him share our story and how we met with his Aunt and Uncle on their 35th anniversary.

Chapter 1

Marriage, Bonding, and Connecting

When you first get together; it's all loving, bubbling, filled with joy, fun, silly, bonding, running behind one another, and can't wait to see one another after work. How many know, in most cases, it doesn't stay that way? Yet, it should. Most couples forget that what is required to attract your mate, is the same thing needed to keep your mate. It's important to build a solid foundation in the beginning because when the storms of life come, they will try to shake the very core of your foundation. Many will be the first to say "oh no not my marriage it's perfect." NEWSFLASH! If you or your spouse are not perfect; how can your marriage be perfect? We must understand that it is not our job to change a person. We must approach the relationship with the understanding that we are two imperfect individuals coming together as one in unity and in covenant with God. As we love, respect, accept, and celebrate each other; we are building a marriage on a solid foundation. If we go into a marriage with expectations to change a person; more than likely, you will be disappointed and this is an open door for strife, bitterness, and frustration to enter into the marriage. When that first disagreement or argument occurs; because the door has already been opened due to the disappointment of expectations that were not met; this is the perfect ground for everything to go haywire! What started out as something really small now has the potential to be blown out of proportion. So you ask yourself, "what do I do, do I yell and fuss until there is an agreement or do I wait until the storm blows over and approach the situation calmly?" *James 1:19 says "My dear brothers and sisters, take note of this: Everyone should be quick to listen, slow to speak and slow to become angry."* I have learned from experience two wrongs don't make it right and it will continue to build a bigger mountain than necessary. It's not about being right or getting your opinion across. In order to weather the storm; the main thing should be to sit down to communicate and compromise if necessary. Make the main thing the main thing, decide to come to an agreement, and refuse to allow the enemy any access to what God has put together. Speaking of giving the enemy access; everybody isn't supposed to be in your business! How many times have we got mad at our spouse and stormed off and went and made a phone call to someone that will take sides? That my friend is not a wise move. Let me be clear; I'm not saying we can't call anyone to vent; however, make sure you choose a person who does not take sides, will be there to listen and provide Godly counsel. ***Proverbs 15:22 states "Without counsel purposes are disappointed: but in the multitude of counselors they are established."*** Instead of holding it in; practice releasing your thoughts in a healthy way. Sometimes words are exchanged and has the ability to trigger old wounds that have not been healed.

Marriage is a special bond between two people who fall in love and have come to an agreement that it is for the long haul. Rather it be through the ups and downs, and even the worst of times, their mind is fixed and determined to make it work.

I'm not saying stay with someone who is abusive because that's not love at all. However, there is nothing like being able to be with that person when they show you themselves, when they show you their awesome side along with their struggles and you know that no matter what; you can feel like royalty in your house even when you don't have it all together. Women, your husband should feel like a king at all times and men, your wife should feel like a queen at all times regardless of the circumstances. Both should know that throughout the day; each other is covering each other and their household in prayer.

During my marriage; there were times when I felt like there was a distance between us and that he was tuning me out and not listening to me. I had to come to an understanding that he was listening to me; yet in his own way. A good marriage understands that even though we are married to each other; we still must respect each other's differences. Marriage consists of two different individuals who do not operate the same way, think the same way, argue the same way nor love the same way. Yet, we know that we are in this marriage together and each of us have faults and make mistakes; but that does not mean the end. We have to learn to work with one another, understand and be patient and know we are two imperfect people striving together each day. It's really easy to be all loveable when things are going smoothly, but soon as it gets hot and heated, we still need to be loveable during the process and step aside and allow God to be God. **Psalms 62:6** declares **"He only is my rock and my salvation, my fortress; I shall not be shaken."**

I remember someone said at a conference I was attending *"duck and allow God to work on him and you get out of the way."* We don't have to prove our point or try to make things right. That was one of my issues-I was always trying to be Ms. Fixer. I'm trying to figure it out and I call myself fixing things; but only to find myself getting in the way instead of letting and allowing God to be God. And in doing that; God showed me Me! Everything was not my husband's fault. I, too, contributed and it took God to show me what I was doing wrong. The Bible declares that God is 'no respecter of persons' and He is a God that will never change. All we need to do is ask Him to direct us and He will give us directions. *Jeremiah 33:3* says *"Call to me, and I will answer you, and show you great and mighty things, which you know not."*

Transparent Moment: Began to call on God and ask Him to show you areas where you need change.

_____

_____

_____

_____

_____

_____

_____

_____

_____

_____

_____

_____

_____

_____

_____

_____

_____

_____

Many times, I've called family or friends when I was going through and needed to talk. But one day, I said *"enough is enough! If I'm getting tired of hearing myself; I can only imagine what they are saying on the other end!"* I started riding out and having conversations with my Father and letting Him know how I was feeling. Other times, I would cry out, scream, or just jam to my music. There were days when all I would do is stretch out on the floor in His Presence. There was no ritualistic way of doing it; it was however I was feeling at the present time. Taking a long drive did a sister good. Either way, I felt so much better. God met me at my level of expectation. Was it easy? No! When you are going through the pain and feeling like things are hopeless; you feel empty and begin to question yourself, but that's when we have to be still and know God is in control. For the most part; you cannot trust your emotions and never allow negativity to enter into your ear gate or your thoughts.

Get Real Moment: Write a paragraph explaining what does your marriage mean to you. If you could change anything; what would it be?

_____

_____

_____

_____

_____

_____

_____

_____

_____

_____

_____

_____

_____

_____

_____

_____

One of the things I changed is when me and my husband was going through; I was not only always trying to fix everything, but I was sitting around worrying and not enjoying who I was in Christ! I was also worried about my husband and what he was doing, which was not healthy.

Philippians 4:6-7 says "Be anxious for nothing, but in everything by prayer and supplication, with thanksgiving, let your requests be made known to God; 7 and the peace of God, which surpasses all understanding, will guard your hearts and minds through Christ Jesus"

Please note; when things start happening, instead of trying to fix it and worrying about it, allow God to minister to you, and see what He says about your situation! I've learned that I could have saved myself a lot of headaches. But no, I had to make my demands and force him to talk and figure this thing out, because after all; communication is the best thing, right? Wrong! It is the timing of communication that is right. The Bible states in the book of

Ecclesiastes; there is a time and a season for all things. When we force someone to communicate in our timing and they are not in the mood; they end up spewing bitterness which in turn; causes offense and strife to set in and now the sick cycle of emotional abuse starts if not caught and dealt with. I had to recognize the trick of the enemy and how he was operating in our marriage to attempt to kill, steal and destroy. The Bible tells me in *2 Corinthians 2:11 "Lest Satan should get an advantage of us: for we are not ignorant of his devices."*

Later within that season; my husband told me when I was "in my feelings and trying to force him to talk", he was just trying to push me away. He also advised me to "stop trying to fix things all the time." I've learned that discernment is needed in order to pursue peace. *Romans 14:19(NIV) says "Let us therefore make every effort to do what leads to peace and to mutual edification*."

Doing those early years, we were learning and as we grow together we start learning more about one another. The key is to weather the storm and ride the waves together. Continue to enjoy one another and have those special date nights. Even when you are not on the same page; learn to agree to disagree. *Proverbs 14:1 says "The wise woman builds her house, but with her own hands the foolish one tears hers down."*

It's a process! It's not an overnight fix. No matter how long you have been married; rather it is 1 day, 3 years, or 20 years or more! You must always allow quality time in your marriage. Still away and have that time of bonding and fellowship. And women, let me tell you something. Don't wait until he plans something! Take the initiative to plan something special....just because. Even if he never does it; still do it. It's called 'sowing into your marriage.' I remember a time when I checked into a nice hotel in town. I began to set up the room with music and romance. I packed an overnight bag for both of us and made sure that the music was on auto play. I told my husband not to plan anything cause my family was visiting from out of town and that I wanted him to meet them. When we arrived at the hotel, he didn't expect anything. When we got to the room, I advised him that I had the key and we could wait until they get back. When I open the door; he heard the music playing and saw the setup and I told him that I did all of this for him. He was so amazed. I didn't do this when everything was going great. This was done in the beginning during our rocky times. I often look back during those times and shake my head and thank God for His faithfulness. His mercy endures forever! Later that month, we had a meeting with our Pastor and out of the blue, our Pastor said Sis Hair, Deacon Hair told me how special you made him feel, you did a weekend surprise getaway for him. If I didn't know how appreciative he was, this definitely was confirmation. We never know how God is changing things within our marriage, we can only trust Him and I am a living witness that trusting

Him is easily said than done. It takes perseverance and endurance. ***Galatians 6:9 declares "Let us not lose heart in doing good, for in due time we will reap if we do not grow weary."***

Chapter 2

Speak Life Onto Your Marriage

I look back and remember when I was going through rocky times; sleepless nights, pacing in the middle of night, crying, and just plain confused! Oh, how I hated every moment of that feeling. It was like someone cut me in my stomach with a sharp knife causing a deep pain with feelings of doubt and hopelessness. Yet, through my cries, prayers, continuing to stay in the word of God, writing in my journal when I didn't feel like writing; even though the days and nights were dark and weary; I knew God was not a man that He shall lie nor would His word return void.

I continued to seek Him and surrounded myself with the right people to minister to me and encourage me. It was when I surrendered my all to God, every step of the way, day by day, minute by minute; I began to find my strength. It was not a feeling; it was a knowing. I knew who I was in the Lord. This did not happen overnight nor did it happen in a week or in a month; it happened in God's timing. I believe it could've happened sooner, but I must admit I was in the way. Sometimes we can prolong what God wants to do by being "Holyghost Jr" and trying to fix things. Then there are times when we give God our worries and then take them back, give God our worries and then take them back and there must come a time when we realize that the battle is not ours; it belongs to the Lord. God gives us the authority to change the atmosphere and our situations. When we speak in agreement with what Father is speaking, creative power is released for the fulfillment of His plans. *'For no word from God will ever fail.' (Luke 1:37)*

There is life-giving impact when we speak, pray or declare words of deliverance, healing and restoration, over our husband, our marriage, and our situations and over ourselves. Take this time and begin to make declarations & affirmations.

The enemy wants you to believe that you don't have options. As a child of God, that can be the furthest thing from the truth. We don't have to walk in a "giving up" spirit with feelings of hopelessness and defeat. Wives', we can make declarations over our husbands that he is a man of God, he is the priesthood of our household, he is the king of our household, and he loves his bride like Christ loves the Church. We must continue to speak those things as though they were; not as they are. It's like when you go to a water fountain, you don't expect soda or ice tea to sprout up. You expect water. So what do you expect out of your marriage? Take a few minutes and begin to think about what you expect and write them down. (writing the vision and making it plain)

_____

_____

_____

_____

_____

_____

_____

Father I thank You that our marriage is lining up according to Your Divine order and nothing or no one can come between our marriage or hinder what You have for us. The tongue has the power of life and death, and those who love it will eat its fruit.

(Prov. 18:21)

Begin to seek The Holy Spirit who is The Comforter to comfort you, The Teacher to teach you, and The Counselor to guide you like only He can. *John 14:16, Jesus declares "And I will pray the Father, and He will give you another Helper, that He may abide with you forever."*

Romans 8:26 Likewise the Spirit also helps in our weaknesses. For we do not know what we should pray for as we ought, but the Spirit Himself makes intercession for us with groaning's which cannot be uttered.

God is so good! He let us know even when we don't know what to pray for! He let us know not to worry and He has you covered! Who wouldn't serve a God like that? I feel a shout right there!!!!

Chapter 3

Forgiveness

What's love got to do with it? What's commitment got do with it? What's sacrifice got to do with it? What's forgiveness and forgetting about it got do with it? What's giving of yourself got to do with it? What's letting go and surrendering got to do with it? Can you honestly and truthfully answer these questions within your marriage? When we forgive; we must also be able to forget. When you forgive one another; you shouldn't keep bringing it up when you get upset or if they do it again. I compare it to when going to God and asking for forgiveness; God does not remind us of our faults. He forgives us and does not ever bring it back up again.

Colossians 3:13 says "Forbearing one another, and forgiving one another, if any man have a quarrel against any: even as Christ forgave you, so also [do] ye." Forgiveness is not for no one else. It is for ourselves. It helps us during our healing process. If we choose to hold on to it; bitterness, resentment, anger, and frustration will begin to settle in. By choosing to forgive; it allows the opportunity to get real with God and get real with ourselves and make a confession~ *"God this is something I need to let go and allow You to work within me and help me to forgive and forget."* There were times in my marriage where the pain was so excruciating; it seemed as if someone was cutting me with a knife. With God; I was able to not only forgive in word; but also forgive in deed. I totally released it and gave it to God. This couldn't have been done without His Grace which is sufficient. In my weakness, His strength was made perfect.

1st Peter 3:1 states "Wives, in the same way submit yourselves to your own husbands so that, if any of them do not believe the word, they may be won over without words by the behavior of their wives." This verse ministers to me all the time because it reminds me & helps me to understand no matter what is going on between my husband and I; my actions of love and supporting him shows the love of Christ. In the midst of what is going on; it cannot be stressed enough that neither person is perfect. When it comes to Jesus Christ; no sin is bigger or smaller than the other. The Bible declares in **Psalms 133 that the blessing dwells where there is unity.**

Yet, forgiveness and forgetting is one of the biggest problems within a marriage. **Ephesians 4:32 (NIV) states "be kind and compassionate to one another, forgiving each other, just as in Christ God forgave you."**

What does forgiveness mean to you personally? What effect will un-forgiveness have in a marriage? Take a moment and answer those two questions and after you've answered them; put down the importance of forgiving one another and going the extra mile of not just forgiving but forgetting. One of the things we can ask the Holy Spirit to help with is forgiveness and being able to forget. The last thing you want to happen while surviving the storms of marriage is to bring up something that you have forgiven your spouse for; yet you can't seem to let it go. I know from a past experience when my husband and I battled the storm of infidelity; I would have just forgiven him however; I wouldn't have forgot about it. But because I realized I needed to heal and allow God to restore and minister to me; I chose to allow God to help me forget. I didn't want to be the one that hindered the healing and restoration of our marriage. Did I struggle? Yes! I went through the comparing myself, and asking what was wrong with me, or our marriage for him to step out. There were moments that were so painful. The forgiveness was easy because of God. Yet, what happens when infidelity happens again with the same person? I had major trust issues. I had to deal with thoughts of *'is he really going where he says he going,'* what about when the phone rings? I would think to myself *'is it her or someone else.'* I found myself getting so caught up in worrying and allowing negative energy pull me in directions that I didn't need to be pulled in. It wasn't until one night in prayer God said to me "Trust Me, don't worry about trusting him and what he is doing, Trust Me." Did the change happen overnight? No, it did not. In the process of God's timing; I backed off and watched God work. As I sincerely placed my trust in God; I watched as He slowly provided inner healing and restored my trust in my husband. One of the things I remember telling my husband is I wanted him to change for himself and for God, not for our marriage. God is the God of the impossibilities! When man says not so, God says it is so! ***Mark 10:27 states "With man this is impossible, but not with God; all things are possible with***

God." Take the limits off and walk through the storm with an expectation that you will see a rainbow on the other side. Continue to enjoy the process and know that God has it under control.

I can say through our 29 years of marriage and being together over 30 years; we have been through ups and downs, curves, hiccups and mountains. But through it all; I would not trade our marriage or be with anyone other than my husband. During the pain and not understanding; God gave me peace and strength. It wasn't easy, it wasn't overnight, nor was it within months when change took place within our marriage. It took well over a year. God had to do a work in both of us because we are only as good together as we are individually and I must admit; we both were a mess. I must testify that God was there with every step that we took together and as He did a 'work' in each of us individually. He gave me family,

Leaders, and friends that was supportive to both of us; not being one sided. I believe this to be the 'key' to all relationships. It is not about proving who is right or who is wrong. There must be a time as mature adults where we are no longer keeping score; but love the agape love like God. Even in times when you don't like your spouse and you want to push them out the bed and snatch all the cover! Ask the Holy Spirit to help you. He is our Comforter and Helper. In those times when you can't handle how you are feeling and it's not a praise that you got to get out; it's pain and anger. I suggest you do what I did. Find your prayer closet and yell, cry, scream, do whatever needs to be done to allow God to begin the healing and deliverance process. Ask Him to send the ones that He has assigned for this season in your life and remove and block the ones He did not. During our marriage; I had some friends tell me to leave my husband. Not because they didn't like him, but they didn't like the pain I was going through. But through the process of healing and restoration and bonding of love, I saw God's hand move on those that had spoken negatively against my marriage! Each one of my friends at different times came and said I want to apologize. I asked what for; because I didn't know. They told me I'm glad you stayed and did not leave. Now it gets even better because none of the people that apologized knew each other; nor did any of them know what the other person had said! I told them that I understood and that I still loved and respected them; but look at God! Won't He do it! To Him be the glory! It was Him that gave me and my husband the strength. I had some friends ask how did you forgive and love like nothing happen? All I could say is 'God did it" and that I remember the man I married. It takes more than just love because sometimes we fall out of love and get angry. It takes commitment and having the determination that says no matter what; we are in a lifelong commitment, unless you are in a dangerous and abusive relationship which is another book! I hear you saying "is it that easy?" No, it is not; however, Phil.4:13 declares that all things can be done through Christ who strengthens you. There will be times when you've tried everything and it still doesn't work. Don't beat yourself up! The battle is not yours; it's the Lords. I remember when He woke me up one morning and said in a still small whisper "The Battle is not yours, it's Mine." Take a moment and reflect on this statement – *'**The Battle Is Not Mine, It Belongs to God.***

_____

_____

_____

_____

_____

_____

If there is any area of struggle within your marriage; begin to seek God and ask Him to show you what needs to be done so that it can be confronted and dealt with. Begin to seek scriptures in those areas and apply them daily. Making the word of God a priority in your marriage is a necessity because the enemy does his job well and we need to do ours by standing on the promises of God! This is what helped me and still helps me today. The word strengthens and sustains and does not come back void.

I remember a story that I was told about a flower bed. We can either keep looking and complaining about what the flower bed looks like by saying what it's not doing, that it's drying up, and the flowers are dying, or we can prune it, water It, and love it even when it doesn't seem like nothing is happening. Before you know it; what was once dead, is now alive. You stopped looking at what it was and start focusing on what it could become. During the rocky times, the flower bed did not sprout the way it was supposed to because no one was paying attention to it. Isn't that sometimes like our marriage? One thing I learned within my marriage is that when we were going through something and my husband continued to make the same mistakes; I was able with God's help to remember the man I married and to know that if that was me; I would want someone to be willing to stick with me. This is when we must realize that we are not wrestling with the person but the spirit behind the action.

Ephesians 6:12 (KJV) states "12 For we wrestle not against flesh and blood, but against principalities, against powers, against the rulers of the darkness of this world, against spiritual wickedness in high places."

In order to weather the storms of marriage; we must immediately find out what the word of God has to say about the situation and start praying against it in the power and authority of Jesus. I'm not going to say that it was it easy and I was always doing it. Matter fact, allow me to be transparent and real about the situation and say No! There were many crying times, I went through the waiting stage, the wailing stage, and every other stage that you could imagine. I thought and asked myself 'was it worth it and was it ever going to change.' I went through so many sleepless and crying nights; yet God and the ones He had assigned in my life to lift, encourage, and to pray for our marriage. Prayer was the key. Did we have naysayers who talked about our marriage? Yes. Were their rumors? Yes. But God!

Each of us have different struggles within our marriage and some people may say I would not put up with that if I was you.

Newsflash! You are not me and you don't know what God has spoken to me about my marriage. I had to learn to surround myself with people that were there for me unconditionally, who gave me their shoulder to cry on, offered their support, and to pray. I had to surround myself with people who had the mindset of not understanding my situation; however, they were there for me regardless of what decision I made. It's not for anyone to decide what they would put up with in YOUR situation. I might not understand; but I will be there for you. It's not for me to decide and tell you what I would put up with. When confiding in someone; you really have to know & understand the character of who you choose to tell. They mean well and they will give advice based on what THEY will do and not what's best for YOU; they often don't won't to see you going through the motions. I had the opportunity to share with both types and had to learn to discern who to give my "ear" to. I had to learn which one allowed healing and growth to continue within our marriage. Learning to go to God and hearing what He has to say about it is the ultimate goal.

Chapter 4

Ask God to Guard Your Heart

John 14:27 declares "Peace I leave with you; my peace I give you. I do not give to you as the world gives. Do not let your hearts be troubled and do not be afraid."

Ask God to guard your heart; especially your ear gate and your eye gate when going through the storms of marriage. We especially need the right influences because of the vulnerable stage we find ourselves in during the pain and not knowing which direction to go and what to do, However, God's Word instructs us: *"Above all else, guard your heart, for it is the wellspring of life" (Proverbs 4:23,).* God knows what He is doing, and He knew there would be reasons for us to guard our hearts. This is why He includes it in His Word. There are many ways to guard your heart in your marriage. In the culture that we live in; whichever way you turn, there is something that is competing for your attention. Social media, reality television,

Facebook, Twitter, Periscope, the list goes on. Let's not even mention the big one.....yep! you guessed it....your cell phone! With this new day and age, people are literally having anxiety attacks when they leave their cell phone home. That's a topic for another book! Cellphones are major distractions especially when you are on date night with your significant other. I remember when me and my honey got together; it was no social media or no cell phones allowed. When we were out, there was no distractions of cell phones; just good ole quality time. I will go as far as saying that it is a necessity and should be a priority between both mates to make and keep quality time with each other. I'm believing for the day when quality time between mates is a priority. This will be a major factor in keeping the divorce rate low. I remember when my husband and I were going through turbulent times in our marriage and he decided to have an affair. I addressed him about it and he kept denying it. That time in my life was so painful and hurtful. I was in total disbelief!

You couldn't have paid me to believe that MY husband; a man whom I have been faithful to, a man that I gave my total heart to; decided to step outside of our marriage and have an affair! No, not my husband, but yes it did happen. During this season of our marriage; it was ups and downs. There were no words that could explain what I was feeling, but God! God guarded my heart and protected my surroundings because it is in this time that you are most vulnerable. Loneliness, feeling out of it, and every other emotion you could think of has the possibility of creeping in. This is when you have to be careful and not receive the wrong advice and end up in places where you don't need to be. I remember my cousin asked me to go out one night and because I love to dance; I said yes. I figured it wouldn't hurt nothing and I needed to get out of the house. I was home just watching TV. When we arrived at the club, I seen faces I hadn't seen in 20 years! The music was playing; yet, I felt within myself an uncomfortableness I had never felt before. I'm sure I stood out like a sore thumb because I stood there holding their coats and purses while they were on the dance floor having a good time! One gentleman came up to me and said "I see you the coat holder for tonight." It doesn't stop there! I spotted a guy who I had a crush on in the 10th grade who was looking gorgeous as ever; comes in and says "Hi Kathy, would you like to dance?" "Yes", I replied. "You still married" "Yes" I responded. He went on to tell me that because he had the utmost respect for my marriage; he wouldn't make a move on me. Ain't that just like the devil? He comes when you are at your weakest and most vulnerable stage. If I didn't know to guard my heart; I could've said "no, I'm not married or "yes", but we going through rough times right now so we can talk." I thank God for guarding my heart during that season. I also can recall another time during our stormy season while I was at work and this guy kept trying to hit on me and it was so noticeable; that people thought that HE was my husband. I'm here to tell you; it is easy to get caught up! This is why it is so important to know who is around you, drown out all distractions, and to seek Jesus Christ daily. I tried so many times to fix my marriage. I tried by expressing and telling him daily how much I loved him. In reality, I had to come to the hurtful truth that I was doing more damage to myself! I had to come to the harsh reality that my husband was only with me physically; not mentally nor emotionally. I could see him getting farther away from our marriage. One day I fixed a romantic dinner; seafood, steak, dessert and I had a nice movie set aside. The table was set beautifully. When he got home from work I was so excited! We ate dinner and afterwards, we watched a movie. While we were watching the movie; out of the blue my husband said "I'm bored" so me not understanding what he meant; I asked naively "what would you like to do?" He replied "nothing, I'm bored with our marriage and I want to separate but I'm going to wait until our son graduate." During that time, our son was in high school and we were 20 years into our marriage. WOW! It felt like someone cut my heart into pieces! Talk about pain and suffering! The man who was my only love tells me this, and that same week I asked him was there someone else and he lied and said that he just wanted his space. What do you do? Confusion hits, hurt hurts in the worse way, you become upset, angry, and then you start to question yourself – "did I do something to cause this within our marriage?" And while all this was going on; in the same week I see my husband transform from one person to a whole different man. His actions were talking! No, his actions were painting a vivid and clear picture. "Ok I told you so now I can put on my best outfit and look good when I leave home, and tell you I will see you later, I'll be back, I'm going out, while you left at home in despair. Continuous tears fell and I was left feeling blank and empty. I could say it was all peaches and roses; but that would be a lie. I did a lot of crying in my prayer closet, seeking God and His word, riding out, a lot of sleepless nights and most times not knowing what to do.

Chapter 5

Peace Be Still

It was during this season in my life where I learned the importance of knowing who to talk to about my problems. I learned to stay away from people who judge and connect with those who not only encourage you; but be a listener also. It is healing to your soul to be able to vent and let out the toxicity that is doing nothing but causing fruits of bitterness and anger to take root. Surround yourself with people who don't give their opinion; but suggest that you seek God! As you begin seeking and pursuing God; you will begin to get clarity due to the inner healing that is taking place. You will begin to realize that you cannot get caught up in the circumstances of what is going on because as a good friend of mine like to say "what you don't value; you will violate. I had to realize that I was not valuing myself by allowing the hurt, pain, depression, and oppression violate the very core of who I was. I had to start loving myself enough to step out of the way and allow God to be God. I remember one-day while in my living room; I was kneeling in prayer and I heard the Holy Spirit ask me *"Is this really working with what you are doing?"* and then before I had a chance to think about it; He responded and said *"No, it is not! Be still and know that I am God!"* This is when I realized I didn't have to do anything but continue to be the wife that I was. I did not have to prove to him nor convince myself of the love I had for him because he already knew that and I knew that. So even while he was out; he still came home to a clean house, dinner, and a non-nagging wife. If I'm asking God to do a work within my husband and renew his mind; I can't be bitter or hateful. I had to allow God to do a work within me and still show love. This was not the time to behave as a foolish woman. *Proverbs 14:1* says *"The wise woman builds her house, but with her own hands the foolish one tears hers down.* It was no longer my responsibility to do what only God could do. I used to hear my husband say all the time that you don't have control over what a person does and you don't have the power to stop them; however, I know that prayer has the power to change things! I also know that The Holy Spirit is a Gentleman and He will not force Himself on anyone. ***Revelations 3:20 says "Behold, I stand at the door and knock. If anyone hears my voice and opens the door, I will come in to him and eat with him, and he with me."*** I would want to tell you it was within months that our marriage began to turn around, but that would be a lie. What I will say even though my husband still did not want to be married; he still maintained our home, still took me out on date nights and was still going to school functions. We were really going through the motions and I had to realize that God will not give you more than you can handle. ***1 Cor. 10:13 says "No temptation has overtaken you except what is common to mankind. And God is faithful; he will not let you be tempted beyond what you can bear. But***

when you are tempted, he will also provide a way out so that you can endure it. It was when I got my eyes off of my relationship and start getting out the way, and enjoying life again. It's like an awakening took place on the inside of me. I remember one of the most difficult things that I had to say to my husband. I said to him "I let you go." Those were the three hardest words I've ever had to say because deep down inside; I wanted him to stay. He never responded nor did he say anything. It is during these times when God will show up and He will always have the right people around to support you. Especially during your quiet time when your mind begins to wonder *'how do I handle this'* you silently ask yourself. During that time of our rocky marriage I felt like I was on a rollercoaster. If you have kids, which we have one; even if you don't argue in front of them, they can tell when things aren't the same. It is always a good idea to sit down and have family meetings to air out anything that is going on within the dynamics of the family by giving everyone an opportunity to express what they are feeling rather it be good or bad. I remember one day my son told me that I was a **door mat.** He was holding on to so much anger because he seen what was going on. I felt the need to explain to him and let him know the truth of what was going on and also keep him lifted in prayer. During the explaining, I never talked against; nor did I bad mouth his father. It's not healthy for the children nor for the family. Every marriage is different; however, God is God and through those times; seek Him and follow His lead. If I learned nothing else while weathering the storms of marriage; I learned to Be Still and know that He alone is God! It was not an easy process nor was it a good feeling. Through the process; God gave me peace and strength. I couldn't look at where my husband was nor could I focus on the circumstances of our marriage. I had to look towards the hills from which comes my help. Did I sometimes get off track by wallowing in my pain? Yes, I did; however, I knew not to stay there because we must pray against distractions. When chaos is going on in your marriage; this is no time to be in your feelings because you are literally in a fight! We must begin to pray and have the understanding that we don't fight against flesh and blood, we are in a fight against spiritual wickedness and demonic activity. *Eph. 6:12-13 (NLT) For we are not fighting against flesh-and-blood enemies, but against evil rulers and authorities of the unseen world, against mighty powers in this dark world, and against evil spirits in the heavenly places. Therefore, put on every piece of God's armor so you will be able to resist the enemy in the time of evil. Then after the battle you will still be standing firm.*

Chapter 6

Finding Yourself

There are times you will feel alone but know you are not. One thing we had to remember is to enjoy life and don't allow self to get lost. So many times couples get lost in the duties of marriage and they forget to enjoy their marriage. It's important to set aside a special day each week rather it be for an hour or two. Put it on the calendar and make sure that it is blocked out. Just as you make someone else time important; remember you are just as important. This is the time when you must learn to say "no" and to officially put that "no" into action; turn off all phones. This is not just time together; this is quality time together. It's your quality time to do something special and fun or just have a one to one with God. Whatever you choose to block that day out for; always keep the main thing the main thing.

I remember my first get away to a women retreat. It was during the stormy times in our marriage; yet I felt so free and relaxed. I was excited because I was finding myself and allowing myself to enjoy life again by not concentrating on my marriage and my husband. I begin doing things for myself. I still maintained things at home, never neglected my marriage, however, I no longer was allowing the issue to absorb me. Prior to me making this change and taking control of the situation; I noticed that when I did allow it to consume me; my looks, and my job performance went down the drain. I was worrying and wondering what was going on. God said in his Word that there is no need to worry and that we can cast all our cares upon Him because He cares for us. I couldn't blame my husband for the way I was feeling; nor for areas I was not doing great in because I allowed that to happen; not him. I was running my own business and had a lot of clients, but the more our marriage grew apart; the more I started neglecting myself. I'm so glad during the process God had certain ones assigned to pray and minister to me and just be a great listener. Was it easy going thru the process? No it was not. It was very painful. As I continually walked thru; I kept my eyes on The Lord and I begin to gradually notice during the process that everyday had just a little bit more peace and everyday had just a little bit more strength than the day before. The Bible declares in *2 Cor. 12:9 "He said to me, "My grace is sufficient for you, for My strength is made perfect in weakness."*

One day while at the Credit Union, I got a call from my husband and he started telling me that he wanted me to know that he must have bumped his head to say that he was leaving a good woman at home. He went on to tell me how much he loved me and cared for me and during the times that he would say hurtful things to me; he was only saying them to push me away. When I got that call I remembered taking the phone from my ear and saying to myself is this my husband? This was nobody but God! Once I stopped trying to fix our marriage and started focusing on God and myself; things shifted. Did it happen overnight? Nope! It happened in Gods timing.

One thing I can say about going through the storm is even through your prayers and studying the word of God; you can't put a timing on your spouse by saying "oh there he/she go again!" No you must stay focus and allow God to be God! No checking his/her voicemails, texting and calling to find out where he/she is at. I'm guilty of all that! I had to realize it was not doing anything to him, it was tearing me down and hurting me, so I had to stop doing that, and put my energy into something else. I'm so glad to know that with God there is nothing impossible. Never lose yourself nor your hope through the ups and downs. Never allow bitterness, anger and un-forgiveness to settle in your spirit; it doesn't hurt them it hurts you. I am not saying that you are not going to get upset because you will; however, it doesn't have to stay in your spirit. ***Ephesians 4:26 (NLT) says "And don't sin by letting anger control you." Don't let the sun go down while you*** *are still angry*." Let God lead you every step of the way. Every marriage may have different issues and problems; but God is the same today, yesterday, and forever and He alone has the right solution for YOUR marriage! Never allow yourself or your marriage to be compared with someone else marriage. Your marriage is unique and special as you are unique and one of kind. God made each of us different, and in our marriage, we can celebrate the differences and enjoy the ride. Will you come against some speed bumps, curves, hills and mountains? Yes, you will. So, I hear you asking yourself '*what do I do when those things happen or what can I expect?*' I'm glad you ask! I can't tell you what will happen or what to expect; but I can tell you who can – the Holy Spirit! The Holy Spirit can show you ways to support and understand your spouse all while showing the love of Christ. He can also teach you how to keep your own personality while loving your spouse and supporting their needs without you abandoning your needs and losing yourself! Yeah, the Holy Spirit can do all that AND some! Continue to look to Christ and not your spouse and know that miracles are happening behind the scenes even when it doesn't look like it. God is shifting, lifting, breaking and dismantling all the forces of hell on your behalf.

Chapter 7

God Is In The Midst!

Zephaniah 3:17 declares "The LORD your God is in your midst, a mighty one who will save; he will rejoice over you with gladness; he will quiet you by his love; he will exult over you with loud singing"

Nobody wants to see your marriage work more than God and the above scripture declares that He will rejoice over you, He will quiet you with His love, He will exult over you. Exult is defined as ***show or feel elation or jubilation, especially as the result of a success***. That's something to get excited about! We are walking by faith and not by sight. There is so much to your marriage! More than you can imagine or think. ***Eph. 3:20 states "Now unto him that is able to do exceeding abundantly above all that we ask or think, according to the power that worked in us.*** Wherever your marriage is; I don't care if it is next too impossible with no thoughts of ever making it work; God can and will meet you right where you are! If God be for you, who can separate it? You can! In our humanity; sometimes we get so caught up and forget to share or tell one another how we really feel. We don't think about it until problems build up and we explode and say something that we end up regretting. To have a successful marriage; always take time to ask God to give you the right timing to speak to your spouse concerning your feelings or concerns. If not; it probably won't be a great conversation. I know because I have been there and done that! God placed this book in me to give you tools to put in your toolbox so that you can avoid the mistakes that I made within my marriage.

I know that God is a Deliverer, a Healer, and a Restorer! He is the Great I Am! No thing is impossible for Him. He can turn the impossible into the possible. He will meet you right where you are! The question then becomes 'do you think YOUR situation is too hard for God to turn around? Are you willing to be patient while He works in His timing and not yours? Are you willing to speak life over your marriage even when it looks dead and hopeless? Whose truth are you going to stand on? Your circumstances and what they look like or God's Word and what He says? I knew you would choose God's Word...just the simple fact that you are reading this book lets me know that you have not lost our hope!

While you are weathering the storm; enjoy life and stay focus! A good idea would be to start a journal so that you can pen the process and have something written to reflect on the progress as you begin to check off every manifested promise. It is critical to not allow negative energy pull you into doubting yourself or what God is saying about your marriage. *Matthew 19:6 says "So they are no longer two, but one flesh. Therefore, what God has joined together, let no one separate."* This is one of the scriptures I stood on while surviving the storm of a turbulent marriage. I anchored onto the word of God and wasn't letting go. To this day; I am still holding on! I'm still writing in my journal and writing letters of encouragement to myself. The Book of Habakkuk tells us to 'write the vision and make it plain.' Let's stop and take a moment and think of words of encouragement that can be repeated daily. Words like *"girl you are fearfully and wonderfully made", "you are more than a conqueror in Christ Jesus," "I have been accepted in the Beloved"* are just a few of the words I write to myself as I remind myself that there is nothing impossible for Him. He will meet you at your level of expectation. I can't stress this enough; it doesn't matter how bad the situation may seem. God has a way of resurrecting dead things! Allow Him to speak to you, and know what He is saying about Your marriage. Marriage is a lifelong learning experience. I always say a person can stick with you when you got everything together, no hiccups or mistakes; but when things get little rough ok, I can do it, then a little rougher ok, but when it gets hot and you ask yourself who is this person I married? All you can ask is for is that God give you strength and help you to be the wife, prayer warrior, and helper for your husband.

Now, can we keep it real? I was at women conference and one of the speakers was telling us how her husband was, how bad their marriage was and how she went into prayer about him. She prayed about all the things he was not doing right, and after she got done, God asked her what about yourself? She replied "I'm a good wife it's him." The words God spoke to her stunned her. God told her to 'get her eyes on herself and off her husband, and while I'm working on you; I'm also working on him. She said she kept her eyes off her husband like God told her to and God turned it around. It wasn't overnight, but nevertheless; He turned it around! I think sometime we expect it to happen overnight. Not saying that it can't happen overnight; however, there is usually a lifelong lesson to be learned in the midst of going thru.

Get Real Moment

How do you react when things in your marriage aren't going the way you feel it should after you been praying and fasting, and it's been a month?

Be honest as you think and write it down. Also, find a scripture in the Bible that you can stand on regarding your marriage.

_____
_____
_____
_____
_____
_____
_____
_____
_____
_____
_____
_____
_____

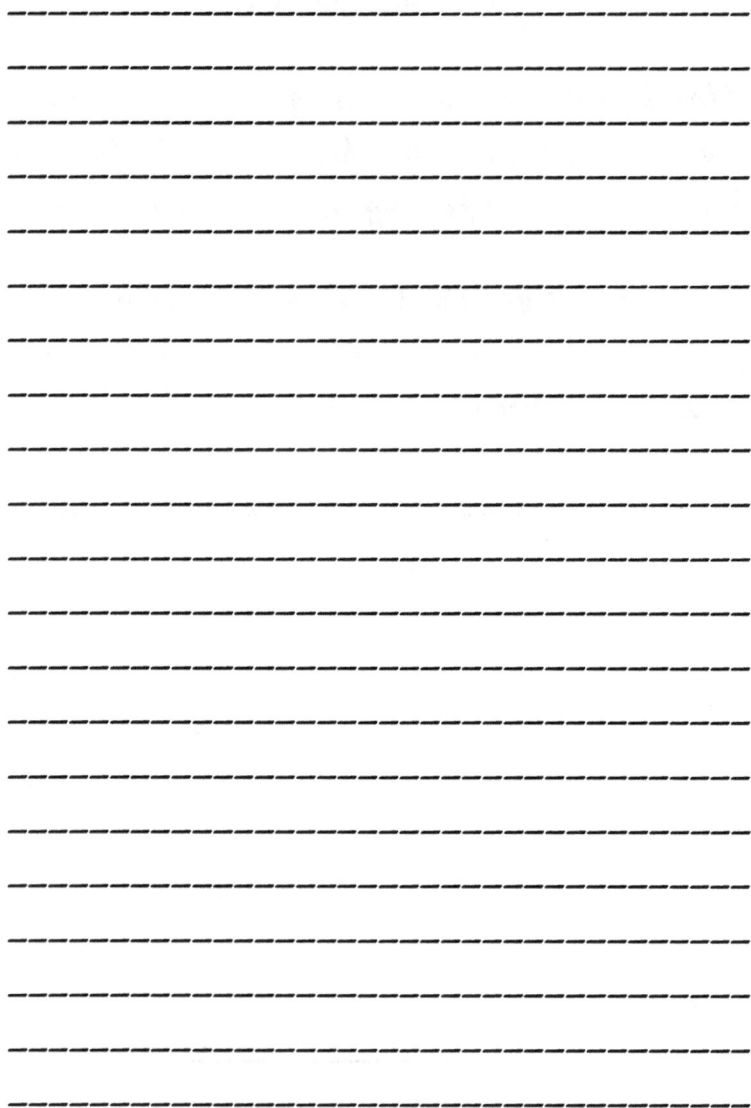

Marriage is a beautiful union between two imperfect people coming together as one. As I reflect on my marriage; I realize that from the moment we exchanged vows between one another; we were in the midst of a learning process. At times; there was lots of enjoyment and laughter and then other times; there was a lot of arguments and hurt. There were even times when we could not stand to look at each other! Yet, through all of the craziness; I was able to realize I have my faults and my spouse has his. I recall a time when I had to keep checking the mail because I didn't want my husband to get the bills and see how much I was using the credit cards and causing unnecessary debt. I was so nervous! I finally made up my mind and told him. Can I tell you that day was like someone took a ton of bricks off of my shoulders! He assured me that it was ok and not to worry about it. I said all of that to say it's not always the man's fault. We have to be honest, transparent and real with ourselves and acknowledge our faults and issues.

Chapter 8

Restoration

While God is behind the scenes making visible what is not visible in your marriage; may I suggest throwing a praise party and thanking Him in advance! *James1:2 (NIV) declares "Consider it pure joy, my brothers and sisters, whenever you face trials of many kinds."* Counting it all joy not because of going through, you're celebrating and having joy because you know your Father is working things out! *Hebrews 11:1 (NIV) Now faith is confidence in what we hope for and assurance about what we do not see.* Continue to know who you are in the Lord and what your worth and value is. Never think you are a failure or when you mess up in your walk as a spouse. It is imperative to always remember that we are in the process of being perfected and there are things that Christ is working out within each of us. While going through our struggles of infidelity; I was still the wife at home praying and taking care of the home. I spoke to the man of God that I knew him to be; not to his actions. I was speaking those things as though they were, not for what they were. Yelling and complaining would not have done any good. I will admit I did question him and attempt to find out what was going on; but it came to a point where I had to step aside and let God be God. Remember earlier, I said that he was just staying until our son graduated. He also told me that by him leaving; it was not my fault. He told me that he was leaving everything to me, that I would be well taken care of; and he also paid off all of the bills. Through all the craziness; he never stopped taking care of home; regardless of what he was doing in the streets. I remember a time when we were having anniversary dinner and in his prayer; he prayed and thanked God for our marriage. Now mind you; this was during the time that he wanted to separate. There is a scripture in the Bible that says 'out of the abundance of the heart; the mouth speaks.' Every marriage is different and can't no one say what you should do in your situation or what you should tolerate. Hopefully, you are not a mat for someone to walk on or settling to keep from being lonely. That is an entirely different book and if you are in this type of situation; I suggest Christian Counseling as soon as possible. For everyone else; seek God through His Son Jesus Christ for direction and Be Still and Know that He Is God!

Healing Prayer

Father I thank You in advance for each woman that is reading this book, as You are ministering to them right where they are at, knowing that there is nothing impossible for You Father, You can turn a situation around that seems like there is no hope cause You are our Healer, Deliver and Restorer, You are The Great I Am, I thank You Father for total peace, strength, and courage for that young lady that feel like she cannot go on, and feel like throwing in the towel, Father I thank You for that person You have assigned in each of their lives and removing and blocking the ones You did not, Father there is no marriage or person You cannot turn around, Father thank You for the foundation and strength of each person's marriage and knowing that no matter what it looks like or feel like, You are their Strength, The Holy Spirit is their Comforter, Teacher, Guidance and Helper! Father, You said You would never leave us nor forsake us, You will be with us to the end, thank You Father that she will not lean to her own understanding, but trust in the LORD with all thine heart; in all thy ways acknowledge You, and You shall direct thy paths. As you continue to guide and give her the plan for her specific marriage, thank You father as she cast all her cares upon You because You care for her and her marriage and what she is going through, thank You Father for the healing process that is taking place in each person and the testimonies that will be coming forth after reading this book, It is my prayer that this book provides a supernatural release of hope, provide supernatural strength, and allows each woman reading this book to be as transparent as I was in writing it. It is my prayer that each person reading this book have a paradigm shift in their thinking and fight FROM victory, not FOR victory! I declare that each person reading this book is more than a conqueror through You whom loves her. She is walking in her purpose and Your Will Father. Her marriage is blessed and she will only speak what thus says the Lord. She shall walk by faith and not by sight. Thank You in advance Father for what is taking place now in her and her marriage as You blow a Refreshing wind of revival upon them; For that woman who is getting married; thank You Father for that foundation and support team that You have assigned before the foundations of the world. I seal this with the wonder working power of The Blood and the name that is above all names; Jesus Christ. Amen

"The change takes place with us first"

Psalms 37:5 Commit thy way unto the LORD; trust also in him; and he shall bring it to pass.

Be the change that you want to see!

NOTES

.